T0123466

climbing
MATAFAO

Stan M. Carter

Edited by:
Amber Spencer
Educator, Language Arts; B.S.Ed.

Inspiring Voices®
A Service of **Guideposts**

Inspiring Voices books may be ordered through booksellers or by contacting:

Inspiring Voices
1663 Liberty Drive
Bloomington, IN 47403
www.inspiringvoices.com
1-(866) 697-5313

Because of the dynamic nature of the Internet, any web addresses or links contained in this book may have changed since publication and may no longer be valid. The views expressed in this work are solely those of the author and do not necessarily reflect the views of the publisher, and the publisher hereby disclaims any responsibility for them.

Any people depicted in stock imagery provided by Thinkstock are models, and such images are being used for illustrative purposes only.

Certain stock imagery © Thinkstock.

ISBN: 978-1-4624-0527-5 (sc)
ISBN: 978-1-4624-0528-2 (e)

Library of Congress Control Number: 2013901858

Printed in the United States of America

Inspiring Voices rev. date: 1/30/2013

For Misty Marie, my best friend, companion, and wife, without whom, this book would never have been written! "We'll always have the Moon!"

Beams of Hope

Oh, moon so pure and bright,
With captivating face,
Your stories bound in space,
Stir love within, this night.

Beneath consoling skies,
As mind and orb embrace,
The heavens precipitate,
With tears of love denied.

The mighty become weak,
When caught within your spell,
What stories would you tell,
If lips were yours, to speak?

Did Galileo's Scope,
Gaze upon your strength,
Or comprehend the length,
Your beams do shine in hope?

Table of Contents

Climbing Matafao

"A man should stop his ears against the paralyzing terror, and run the race that is set before him with a single mind." Robert Louis Stevenson

Preface

Jules Verne's account of man's *Journey to the Center of the Earth* by climbing into a volcanic cone in Iceland became a big screen epic in 1960. Kids in theaters everywhere crawled into the screen with Pat Boone and James Mason to explore the Earth's interior. My boyhood fascination with such explorers sparked an imagination that demanded answers, led to a career in science, and precipitated my acceptance of a teaching position on a small Pacific island. Surrounded by volcanic peaks in a tropical paradise, the jungle soon entangled me with adventures. Climbing Matafao recounts the dangers faced and obstacles overcome while trapped on a volcanic mountain with three of my students in the Samoan Islands. A story written at the request of my students, and at last, recorded for young readers everywhere.

Investigating Volcanic Vents 1

"Oh-h-h! Oh-h-h-h! Oh-h-h-h-h!" The cry from behind yanks my head around, as it becomes more and more faint against the waterfall's roar.

"Where's Joey?" I yell, turning to TJ and Sean. Eyes bulging from disbelief, ghostlike they turn and look down the slope of the mountain into the jungle. My head swims in a pool of fear as I quickly move to the site of a fresh mudslide.

"Joey! Joey!" I scream over the now monstrous roar of the waterfall. But as I listen intently, the green envelope of darkness below echoes only the scream of silence.

"What if Joey's unconscious; what if he's broken an arm, a leg, his neck? Oh God, what if he's dead!" I

gasp. *"How will I get down there; how will I get him out? What was I thinking, bringing kids on top of this volcano?"*

What causes a person to fearlessly climb a precipice until it has him entangled in its snare? Is it a throwback to some kind of primal curiosity? Consider the octopus that climbs into a jar, but refuses to abandon his discovery, even as he is reeled into an outrigger by the noose around the jar's neck. Or perhaps, it's the way a person is nurtured, always being dared to attempt the impossible, until the daring voice is inside their own head.

Having grown up in the Ozark Mountains, the grandson of men who pursued their fortunes mining beneath the surface, I was no stranger to forest or danger. Many times, as a boy, I had crawled into the earth's darkness as a spelunker of caves, or lost direction while following deep Ozark ravines. Such adventures, a seventh grade book report, and perhaps a special feature at a little hometown theatre may have fueled this drama atop a volcano six thousand miles from those hills.

Could a captivating watercolor in a small plain hardbound book in seventh grade really have inspired such a journey? Natives clad in leaf and vine, poles atop their muscular shoulders, carry the lifeless body of a noble-looking man. The jungle pathway ahead winds uphill toward a volcanic peak that breaths fire into the sky. Below, a few words share the story of the Samoans' love for this man who lived among them for much of his life. Now, carrying out his last wish, they take him to his burial site atop this volcanic mountain near his island home. The man was Robert Louis Stevenson, the book his own *Treasure Island*, and the reader, a goofy kid who has now gotten his own students lost in the jungle atop a Samoan volcano.

Teaching in the same islands, I stared through walls of open weave wire from my tin-roofed classroom at the perfect volcanic cone on the slopes of Matafao. Though the wire kept the rats and insects of the tropics out, the view constantly drew my attention into the distant volcanic peaks that lined the horizon. Day after day, I read *Treasure Island* giving every character his own distinct voice. My students listened intently as pirates sailed in search of buried treasure, with adventure oozing off every page. Day after day, beyond the wire, Matafao beckoned me to come and see what adventures she held. But, when I asked what I might find there, my students always responded, "Nobody goes up there, Stanley!" And that made the voice in my head dare me all the more.

Matafao, "the eye of the needle," has the shape of a sewing needle all right, but what fascinated me was the volcanic cone that protruded from her side. It was easy to imagine her breathing fire and magma, as she grew out of the ocean, forming this small island thousands of years ago. As I stared at her outstretched arms that meander to the ocean below, she seemed to entice me with the very words of the adventures I read. Like the cowardly lion at the witch's castle from *The Wizard of Oz*, I would point and jest: "I'm going up there! I might not come back alive, but I'm going up there!" And the kids would laugh.

Now, as I look down into this bottomless ravine, those words echo with a foreboding of the fate that entangles me.

This day began, as any great adventure would, with three students, Sean, Joey, and TJ, meeting me at the base of the mountain. Sean, though small in stature, was hugely adventurous in every sense of the word. He was a reader, a storehouse of knowledge. Joey, on the other hand, was the impetuous type, always shouting answers in class, but seldom the ones being sought. He was the clown, a comedy of errors, the one that made each of us take ourselves a little less serious. TJ, like a soldier, stood his ground and proved his worth. Though his presence might be overlooked, he was the glue that bound our troop.

It was going to be a five-hour trek accomplished by simply walking up one of the volcano's buttress-like arms that sprawled down to where we stood in the road. Unlike her distant image, Matafao appeared ten times taller in stature. Her terrain unfamiliar and her dangers unknown, I questioned the boys about the contents of their backpack and their willingness to follow direction beyond the school walls.

"We've got it under control, Stanley." Joey interrupted, trying to prove the point. "Sean brought a pack and all of us have something in it."

"Yeah, we're going to take turns carrying it," affirmed TJ, as he stood to take the pack from Sean, "I volunteered to carry it first,"

After seeing the expression of doubt on my face, Sean bolstered my confidence by saying, "Don't worry, Stanley! I'll keep a close eye on everything in it!"

Then, giving a reassuring smile to my wife, I said, "See you around noon. We'll take an aiga bus." And she drove away with a patronizing smile.

The climb was almost effortless in the beginning, the trail easy to follow. The grade was walkable, but slow in pace. Spirits were high and the boys' stories entertaining, as I cautioned about the conservation of food and drink. *"This is a piece of cake, or at least a cupcake,"* I thought. *"Hmm, what do they have in that backpack?"*

Soon the pathway began to narrow. Only a few feet in width, the trail persisted. I kept wondering, *"How did this trail get here? Is its origin human or animal?"* My knowledge of the island gave me no answers, but the pathway was sure, and we pressed on.

At a halfway point in the climb, the path turned and became extremely narrow with much less foliage. We could see the villages below, appearing in miniature, their palmed beaches and reefs opening into a vast ocean. We stopped for a short break to admire the view and decided to take some pictures for their classmates. Still full of energy, the boys climbed some small fruit trees that sprawled out over the edge of the ravine, in hopes of getting a better look.

"Whoa, look!" Joey announced, dangling at the end of an overhanging limb, "the view from out here is awesome!"

Taking a quick picture at their request, I reeled them in, and thought about destroying the evidence later. At that point, and most likely the cause of my wife's smile, I realized my poor judgment. We were approaching 9:30, and without a miracle, a 12:00 return was out of the question. "*Oh well, it's downhill on the way back; I'm sure it will be faster and easier,*" I consoled myself.

Watching them barter for the backpack, I urged with a smile, "Let's go boys, we still have a lot of mountain ahead."

Thirty minutes further along, the boys began complaining of thirst. Their red faces and perspiration-soaked shirts gave evidence both to the humidity and our struggles. With every step, and without my knowledge, they had been consuming their stash as they followed close behind. As dry within as they were wet without, they now realized their folly.

Earlier on the trail, a coconut crab wearing an African snail shell had crossed our path. The largest terrestrial hermit crab, they actually climb palm trees and cut coconut stems with their largest claw. If the fall breaks the hull open, they have a feast that lasts for days. Prompted by that encounter, I began to look up. *"There are coconut trees ahead and they are laden with fruit,"* I observed, *"but are they the drinking kind?"*

A science teacher's attention to detail would now pay off. Having watched Samoans climb for coconuts, I removed my belt and wrapped it around my ankles like hobbles. Stretching the belt around the tree's trunk, my shoes biting into the bark, I climbed inchworm fashion up some twenty feet to the cache of coconuts. Machete in hand, I swung for the prize; one, two, three, they dropped with a thud! With great restraint, and a forced look of humility, I refrained from beating my chest like Tarzan.

Then came the hard part, getting back down! Bark on some palm trees resembles fish-like scales. Jutting upward in a spiral fashion, they encompass the trunk with knife-like protrusions. Unlike an Ozark elm, you can't just hug the tree with your legs and "shimmy down." Scales like these would first tear at your clothes, and then dig into your flesh. Slowly, I squirmed and wiggled the belt over the protrusions, inching my way down in an attempt not to fall. The boys giggled at my awkwardness, as they watched their white-skinned teacher climb with such caution and fear. They had seen this done with greater agility by Samoans many times before. But their gratitude was evident when, after husking the coconuts, they tipped and drank nectar from the cup-like shells.

After a short rest, we launched ourselves refreshed toward the volcanic cone. As we trekked, my mind wondered what we might find ahead. My intentions on this trip were to simply peer inside Matafao's mouth. I had brought no provisions for going inside, not a single foot of rope. Other than a knife, machete, and band-aids, there was no safety net for unforeseen emergencies.

"I'll just turn around and go back before I'll risk a student getting hurt," I told myself. *"These teenagers, though a little clumsy at thirteen with their big ideas and bigger feet, are the adventurous type just like me... Hmm, come to think of it, that's probably not a good thing!"* So at this juncture, I vowed to keep them close at hand and involved in conversation. *"Perhaps, I can redirect some of that energy and overactive imagination?"* We talked of tattoos, flying foxes, and pirates. My stories of sled riding on snow covered hills were a big curiosity for these South Pacific boys, who would never see it snow.

"I remember the day you talked about snowball fights, and you brought a snowball made out of frost from your refrigerator," Sean recounted with his elephant-like memory.

Hearing that, Joey entertained with, "Yeah, I thought you were going to throw it at me, for sure!"

"Just think," I said with a smile, "this will be your great adventure, one you can tell your classmates, or even your own kids someday."

We laughed, talked more, tried to top each other's stories, and the climb seemed much lighter. TJ was our point man, leading the way. Before we knew it, we were nearing the base of the cone. To our surprise, the trail disappeared and the jungle thickened. We now had to climb over and through limbs, some dead on the ground and others extending down from tropical trees. The boys, while enjoying the jungle challenge, suddenly realized there was no way around the cone.

"Now what'll we do?" Joey asked with a face full of despair, his head falling forward in disgust. But not one of us had an answer.

Formed during a volcanic eruption, this cone had been a vent for spewing out gases and lava. If it still had an opening, it might provide a view into the throat of Matafao. The fact it sits as an inverted snow cone on a steep incline, makes it appear saddle-like on the uphill side. Climbing toward the saddle-horn of the cone from that side, would be a shorter and safer task. But our way up approached the lower side, which dropped into deep and steep ravines on both the left and right.

Face to face, we stared at the cone. Our most dangerous climb towered over us, steeper than anything attempted—until now! What's more, the foliage on its slopes looked more like celery than saplings, as it had appeared from a distance. Still, the boys approached the challenge with square shoulders and pursed lips of determination. Without handholds to support their weight, however, the climb would be too dangerous. This realization, that we might have to go back without even reaching our quest, came as a huge blow to our morale.

Not one to give up quickly, I asked the boys to take a rest, while I tried to scale the face of it. With looks of hesitation, they found a place to sit, as I confronted the cone. Upon inspection and to my surprise, its surface was covered with tailings and a damp black mud. *"I'm used to tailings,"* I reassured myself. *"I've climbed the chat piles of Ozark mines, flown kites from atop them, and sled down them in winter snows. But, this slippery mud formed from eroded lava thousands of feet above the ocean on a steep volcanic cone, not so much!"*

As hard as I tried, the herbaceous plants pulled loose into my hands, and my feet slipped out of place. My muscles began to twitch from the clinch of stiff posturing, and my brow became beaded with the perspiration of fear, coupled with exertion. My brain was tormented beyond its limits.

"If I make it to the top, I still have to get back down," I concede, after climbing some twenty feet up the incline. *"Even if it has never snowed on this South Pacific Island, from up here, the slippery ride to the bottom would be an all-time record for an Ozark sled."*

Not a ride you would likely survive … the image made me shudder. With hands shaking and unsure footing, I descended the slope to the waiting boys.

Though safe at the bottom, a new challenge presented itself. *"How do you tell the boys such bad news after their grueling climb to get here?"* I deliberated, and a distraction came to mind. With great hope, but lacking confidence, I pitched my idea.

"We heard the roar of a waterfall some time back. Maybe, water spews out of the belly of the Matafao from the mouth of a cave?" I baited their curiosity. "We can go back to the sound of the roar, and see if there is an opening into the mountain at that point," I set the hook. With their heads bowed, they rolled their eyes in an attempt to glimpse each others' reaction. Reluctantly, they took the bait; but, I knew when we got there, I'd have to come up with a new plan.

"Guys, it's already noon, but at least we're heading in the right direction—downhill!" I encouraged, knowing their "on top of the mountain feeling" was down in the dumps.

In no time at all, we made it to the point where the sound of the waterfall was the loudest. Holding onto limbs of small trees along the ridge, we peered intently in the direction of the roar, hoping to glimpse a spewing jaw. Then, I heard that chilling cry!

"Joey! Joey!" I yell again, against the roar of the waterfall.

This time, I think I hear a faint reply. "Listen!" I bark at the other two. "We need to know if he's alright!"

Then from the bottom, we hear a definite, "Yeah!" and the boys beam with elation.

Trying to imagine his treacherous slide through dense jungle, I shout, "Are you alright?"

"Yeah, you ought to come down here; it's really neat down here!" he responds as the adventurous explorer, when we were expecting cries of pain.

Feeling air entering my chest again, I finally share the boys' elation. Still, the ominous task of getting Joey back up top, weighs heavy on my mind.

"Can you climb back up?" I bellow out, using my hands as a megaphone.

"I'll try!" he counters with a determined voice.

But one try, after another, fails and dashes the moment's hope. There is only one solution, and not the one I was looking for. I'll have to find a way down.

Near the shore at 7am, TJ, Joey, and Sean
are ready for a Matafao adventure.

Surviving Slippery Slopes 2

What has been a captivating rainforest of beauty, on the upward climb, now looks like a dark hand-dug basement with suffocating webs of danger at its bottom. Thoughts of uncontrolled tumbling, and bones poking out of broken limbs, flash in my head. *"Stop that,"* I tell myself, *"you've got to go down there!"* But my loss of control over our situation, as well as my fear of what lies ahead, has me by the throat. I can't help thinking of my greatest childhood nightmare at this moment. *"It's a nitwit explorer that will walk into a fog-filled bog where "The Creature from the Black Lagoon" waits for him,"* I acknowledge in disgust. *"Now, I'm the nitwit explorer!"*

Images from scary movies start playing in my head, as this familiar backdrop revives their memory. Even though I know they're not real, they still cause my heart to beat wildly. "O*k! You're the adult here, focus on the boys*," I mumble to myself. *"They've never even seen the inside of a movie theatre. This is normal terrain for them… get a grip!"*

After hearing Joey's voice, Sean turns and calmly asks, "How are we going to get him out, Stanley?"

Fortunately, neither of them sense the panic alarms going off in my head. It's good to know my presence is reassuring, at least for them. Maintaining their confidence is essential and just as important as finding a way out of here!

Peering down the ridge, I realize for the first time, the vegetation is not typical rainforest. Growing ever steeper with altitude, the downward sloping arms of Matafao hold onto very little soil. This thin layer can only support small trees and palm-like herbaceous plants. Unlike the giant emergent trees on her lower slopes, this canopy is at most fifteen feet high. The small tree trunks sticking out of the slope below resemble a larger-than-life plinko game, one that now awaits my first move as the puck!

"Maybe I can slide downhill from tree to tree, using each one to break my fall," I reason. *"A few trees are the size of my wrist and have light-colored bark. If they really are woody plants, they could have root systems large enough to stop me."* Though extremely intimidating, this seems my only option … but what about the other

two boys? Hoping to instill confidence, I turn and begin outlining my plan.

"I don't know what the way out, from down there, will look like. You are my safety net. If anything goes wrong, you guys can go for help," I instruct, using my most serious face. "You know the way back down the mountain from here, just follow the same path we came up," I reassure them. "Joey and I will holler from the bottom and let you know how we're doing." They look at me with a troubled stare; then, nod in agreement, as I turn to focus on my first target tree.

Knowing my rear end will act as a break, I lean back as far as I can, shuffle my feet, and begin sliding toward the first white-barked tree. Bracing for impact, the jolt of hitting the first tree isn't too bad. Using my rear to maneuver sideways, I mentally talk my way through it and line up with the next tree. With reassured confidence, I descend rapidly toward the second tree, while exhaling a sigh of relief.

"This is going really well," I think with some pride. Using the same strategy, I attempt a third target and a fourth. However, just as I began to line up for the fifth tree, to my right, I hear a familiar sound in a terrified tone.

"Oh-h-h! Oh-h-h!" It's Sean, passing me in a blur, as he slides down the very same rut Joey made.

"There goes my safety net!" my heart acknowledges

in anguish. *"Can't they listen? Didn't I make myself clear?"* I angrily grumble in frustration.

"Are you alright, Sean?" I shout with anxious anticipation like before.

"Don't worry, I'm ok!" he roars back from the bottom. Luckily, his answer affirms, we have once again survived catastrophe.

"Regroup and calm down," I tell myself, *"this is no time for losing it and scaring kids! We still have a long, unknown road ahead, and it needs to look like fun, at least for them."*

"TJ, can you hear me from up there?" I howl, even as I try to diffuse my anger.

"Yes, I can hear you!" he shouts.

"Change of plan," I console, "we're all going to the bottom of this ravine. No one is hurt, *yet*," I remind him. "We can all go together from down there, but I need you to follow my path. I'll wait right here for you. Do you understand?"

"OK! I get it!" he acknowledges, as if standing at attention, while waiting for direction from the pathway above.

He carefully descends his way to me, one tree at a time. Then together, we systematically pick targets, as we move toward our destination. Sweat-drenched by humidity and mud-streaked from our descent, we arrive in the ravine where Joey and Sean wait. Within minutes, the four of us are sitting together on huge, black volcanic boulders with our feet in crystal clear water, cleaning great globs of mud from our shoes. Giddy from our success, we laughingly relive Joey's fall, the challenges of the slippery slope, and our good fortune.

At the end of our laughter, the roar of the waterfall overtakes our conversation and draws us back into the present. Surrounded by hundreds of tropical plants, giant versions of those found in every household foyer, we resemble hobbits lost in an enchanted forest. Fern-like palms and tropical herbs fan out their glistening damp foliage into a blackish-green labyrinth over our heads. The shadows they paint on the moss-covered floor spread out like giant handprints, with beams of misty sunlight dangling through their fingers. The stones illuminated in the streambed sparkle as if flaked with gold, while calm pockets of dark water, mirror an identical underworld of reflection from below.

Wide-eyed with curiosity and mesmerized by a jungle they've never seen, the boys ask to explore their surroundings. The spring, we're soaking our feet in, flows from the roaring waterfall only a short distance from where we sit. *"They probably want to hunt for buried treasure,"* I imagine, from memories of my own childhood. *"I hope the pirates left a map!"* Looking at my mud-covered watch which reads 12:30, I nod in agreement, knowing my sore muscles wouldn't want me to stand anyway.

Though they find comfort in my reassurances, the fact still remains, I have no idea what lies ahead. In these following few moments, through a self constructed pep talk, I must somehow overcome the whirlwind of doubt that muddies my mind.

Standing next to Robert Louis Stevenson on his volcanic mountain in Western Samoa.

Using rags around his ankles to grip the bark, a Samoan climbs for coconuts.

Creating Courage out of Catastrophe

3

Having lived on Tutuila for seven months, I've had time to see much of this seventeen mile long island. While walking her beautiful beaches and snorkeling her inlets, I have unwittingly stumbled into some difficult situations along the path. Admittedly, this ravine is another stumble. Yet, as I search for the resolve and strength I need, my mind begins to replay the memory of two situations that make Matafao appear small in comparison.

Over Thanksgiving, I had the opportunity to night snorkel for crabs off Coconut Point, the very village we admired on our way up Matafao. Sioni, a friend from the Islands of Tonga, invited me to come along and help spear a Thanksgiving feast fit for a Matai. Steve, another friend who managed one of the fisheries in

Pago Pago, was there during the invitation and asked to come along. Like myself, Steve is a Palagi, a name given the first white explorers who the Samoans thought had dropped out of the heavens. No doubt, some 450 years later, they are absolutely sure we didn't drop from heaven, though they kindly refer to us by the same name.

Meeting one evening, with underwater flashlights and spears in hand, we snorkeled out into the bay. Surprisingly, all the animals that hide in the reef's coral during the day, festively display their exquisite colors openly at night. Like a kid lost in a candy store, I swam out into the ocean with bug-eyed excitement. When I finally surfaced, I was unnerved to discover that I was completely alone.

"Where did they go?" I wondered, looking side to side. Except for the lights on the shore, only the faint glare of a crescent moon was visible on the water's surface. I'd grown up using boat lights to gig fish back home; but didn't realize, underwater flashlights aren't visible above the surface of the water. *"No worries,"* I calmly thought, *"I'll just snorkel toward the shoreline"*. That seemed the safest thing to do. *Yet,* I couldn't help thinking, *"Someone should have had a plan, especially when the adjoining bay is known for its sharks!"*

After a short swim in that direction, I saw something ahead I couldn't explain. It looked similar to a large jellyfish. Swimming closer, to my horror, I discovered it was a group of speared fish on another snorkeler's rope-line. Because sharks are attracted to blood, rope-lines are used to keep bloody fish at a safe distance. This line stretched out over a hundred feet from its owner. Unfortunately, because of my curiosity, I'd swum within a few feet of the blood cloud.

"I've just become shark bait!" I reeled in my head. Making a panoramic look for sharks and gulping a chest full of air, I dove below the surface. Trying not to frantically thrash the water which would also attract sharks, I swam with all my might away from the speared fish. Unknowingly, I was swimming out into deeper waters and came up barely able to stand. By a stroke of luck, however, Steve was standing only a few feet away and smiled when he saw me. *"What a relief, safety in numbers,"* I sighed, before relaying the terror of my misadventure.

But this was Daredevil Steve, who after living on island for more than two years, most likely suffered from island fever. Not really a fever, it's a claustrophobic feeling produced by the perception of being trapped on a small island. No matter how beautiful in the beginning, paradise with its constant temperature, lack of seasonal changes, and ocean confining perimeter can become prisonlike. Many people think shopping malls are fun, but imagine being locked inside one for two years! For those, who have lived in the vast terrains of temperate climates, this sameness can produce stir-crazy boredom and even a living-on-the-edge, testing of limitations. An experienced scuba diver, Steve looked me in the eye and with a comical grin pointed seaward.

"Let's go out to the rocks along the airport runways and snorkel," he dared. "There's bound to be more fish and crabs out there." But in my mind, the airport rocks represented deep-ocean, a terrifying scenario in this darkness.

There is very little flat surface on this volcanic island, certainly not enough for an airport. The Corp of Engineers, years ago, chose to haul mega-tons of rock to the sea shelf in order to build a manmade island. When finished, it had runways long enough to land even the largest planes. Impressive as that sounds, it didn't look like any place I wanted to snorkel: in deep-ocean, with the sharks, and at night! Before I could answer, Steve dove seaward and swam toward the rocks. Engulfed with fear, I panned the horizon. The blackness of deep-ocean glared back at me, accentuated by only a few frothy lines of incoming waves and the distant rocks of the runway.

"Calm down, you can do this!" I told myself, trying to bolster my confidence. Then, due to an overinflated ego, or perhaps the fact I again found myself alone, I followed him. After swimming for a short time, I stopped for a directional check. Observing the rocks in the distance, I thought they looked a little larger, though they didn't appear any closer.

"Objects always look closer than they actually are in open-ocean," I remembered from a lifeguard course. However, nothing in that lifesaving book had prepared me for this. *"How far are those rocks? They must be way the heck out there,"* I guessed. *"Why am I doing this? I have nothing to prove here!"*

Steve was nowhere in sight, as I turned and began swimming for the beach. It dawned on me, we hadn't even agreed on a final meeting place. Keeping up a good strong stroke, I also realized, I would be arriving empty-handed … not one speared crab in my possession. *"Oh well, I have all my limbs, and I'm not suffering from shark bite or blood loss. That's good enough for me!"*

Stopping to examine my success, I again eyed the rocks of the airport. They looked exactly the same, no visible change. Surveying the shoreline ahead, I noticed that it was still a line of very distant lights.

"Pick up the pace!" I determined. And with head down and heavier strokes, I again pulled toward the beach. But after some five minutes, another heads-up check revealed that I was no closer to the shore. *"Time to re-evaluate,"* I reasoned.

"Was the tide going out?" I questioned. *"Was there a rip current where this bay opened into the ocean?"* Letting my feet dangle, I felt for the flow of a current below me. It was definitely there! *"Can I out swim this tide?"* I doubted. *"My only other option is the airport rocks!"*

Then I remembered, the lifesaving book said to swim parallel to the shore, until you swim out of the rip tide. I looked left and right. On my left was another bay that opened into the sea from this same inlet. To my right, I saw coral reef fading off into the night's darkness. Literally stuck between the rocks and a hard place, I convinced myself to swim toward the shore one more time, giving it all I had.

After about five minutes, that felt like an hour of all-out speed-swimming, I stopped to make a quick observation. Nothing, *absolutely nothing*, had changed!

"OK," I contemplated while gasping for air, *"what now!"* Turning over on my back, I began a restful backstroke from a floating position. *"What are my options?"* I deliberated. *"Should I swim in open sea to the airport? Could I climb up the giant boulders that roll out onto the ocean floor?"* Peering over my shoulder, I examine the possibility. *"It doesn't look good! What if this current carried me out to sea, and I missed the rocks altogether? Would anyone know where to look for me in the morning? Would the sharks find me first?"*

After restfully paddling for some time, I rolled my head over and glanced at the rocks. How far had I drifted out of the bay?

"Wait a minute, something's changed!" I discovered. *"It looks like I've moved inland! That couldn't be, could it?"* The image of a raft, caught in front of a small wave and

carried to shore, leaped into my head. My brain began to frantically search for answers. *"There is always a few inches of warmer surface water moving toward land in waves of energy,"* I recite from an oceanography class. *"If water is always going out, water from somewhere has to be coming in,"* I reason. *"Is it really possible, that so little effort could save me?"*

One thing I knew for sure, there was a lot more backstroke where that little effort had come from. With resolve, I shifted gears. Slowly, the rocks of the runways moved from my side and began to disappear at my feet. *"I'm moving! I'm really moving!"* I yelled in my head.

Soon and by some miracle, I was standing chest-deep, walking … as if for the first time. When at last, I arrived on dry ground; although empty handed, my head was filled with screams of elation. Surprisingly, it would be this experience, my own life saved, that would save two others a month later.

Everyone on Tutuila knows one of the most beautiful beaches is on the far side of the island. Sailele beach with its clean sands, beautiful palm trees, and abundant sea life is only 2400 miles from Hawaii and rivals any beach found there. Many of the teachers from our school spend their "your turn with the car" weekends on this beach. Over the Christmas holidays, a small group of us chose to drive to Sailele for a picnic and swim.

Being the only man on this trip, I snorkeled solitarily in

the four foot of seawater that normally covers Sailele's titanic-sized coral shelf. Eventually, I discovered an unusual formation below the coral floor. It was a giant open vault, a hole cut out of the coral bed, that dropped ten feet to the sandy seafloor below. With a nearly cylindrical shape, it was at least twenty-five feet across. Its wall had many openings that led into cave-like tunnels in the coral reef. Each attracted an abundance of sea creatures and one curious teacher. Like underwater aquariums, these tunnels were filled with colorful fish, snails, eels, and starfish. Because of the safety the caverns provided, these cave inhabitants allowed you to come amazingly close before they darted into smaller holes for protection.

Swimming into these aquatic biomes was easy; the difficult part was getting back out. Before you could swim to the surface of the vault for a gulp of air, an inventive backstroke was required. After an hour of exploring, a receding tide made it too difficult to exit the caves and return to the surface. Climbing back upon the reef, I noticed, the only opening for tide water to move seaward was through a top to bottom slit on the open-ocean side of the submerged vault. Outgoing tide water moved through this seam with incredible force. And the coral shelf above, that surrounded the vault, was now covered by a wading depth of less than two feet of water.

A couple of our lady teachers had been snorkeling near some gigantic sea boulders a few hundred feet away.

They had been watching me appear and disappear into the water above the vault.

"What are you doing?" They shouted curiously over the roar of the waves.

"I've been looking at some beautiful fish that live in the caves under my feet," I replied. "But the tide is getting pretty strong." With that said, I turned and walked toward the shore where my wife had motioned for lunch.

As I visited with my wife, the two of them peered into the sunken vault as they walked in the shallow water along its edge. Then, I heard giggling and noticed one had fallen into the hole. While trying to pull her out, the other teacher also tumbled in. Not giving it much thought, because the water level above the vault was only eighteen inches at most, I failed to notice that the tide was pulling them seaward at a rapid rate.

They were swimming and still giggling, but like me, failed to see the danger until it was too late. The outgoing tide quickly pulled them through the slit in the vault. Beyond them, as occurs every day, was a tumbling, swirling wall of seawater where the incoming waves meet the force of the rip tide. Giggles soon turned to cries for help! Although swimming with all their abilities, they were losing ground as they battled against the force of the currents.

The three of us on the beach ran to the edge of the

vault. But by the time we arrived, they were already out of reach, beyond the coral shelf in deep water. Though swimming with a persistent stroke, they were being pulled toward the churning wall of water behind them. As they cried for my help, I felt so helpless. My strength and lifesaving abilities would be no match for the force of the rip current. Diving into the water and attempting to pull them ashore, would only produce more drag by the tide and disastrous results. The fear in their eyes pulled at my heart. Still, that very fear is what causes a drowning swimmer to clamp onto their rescuer, drowning them both.

Their only hope was to do what I had accidently discovered that night at the airport. Rolling over into a restful backstroke, though it might sound crazy, was the only way to come back to shore. But, could I convince them that such a ridiculous move would actually work? Just like I had done, they were swimming with all their might to no avail, losing ground with every stroke.

At that point, I began to plead and beg them to listen to what I was saying. They had to believe and turn, before it was too late. Fatigue was setting in. It was evident in their slowed movements and could be heard in their weakening voices. If they didn't turn soon, I would have no choice but to swim out to them, bring them to surface, and try to float them and myself into shore. They were now becoming too tired to give much resistance. Though I believed it would be a futile effort, I had made my resolve to try!

Miraculously, out of exhaustion, Debbie turned over to a floating position. Although able to exert very little effort, she immediately started moving toward us. We cheered her on, as she began to giggle from a combination of fear and amazement. She was soon over the vault and nearing its edge, where we waited with outstretched arms.

Seeing Debbie's progress, Sharon turned and began a backstroke. In no time at all, she too was coming toward us at a rapid rate. Reaching for Debbie, I caught her hand, and she began to stand. Unfortunately, due to exhaustion and current, she stumbled and rolled on the sharp coral. Nevertheless, we got her to her feet. Right behind her, Sharon grabbed my hand. She also rolled, before we could get her on her feet. Standing side by side, bleeding from cuts on both elbows and shins, they completely ignored their wounds and began hugging each other with tears of laughter.

Although sitting bewildered in this ravine, the recollection of these two events completely overshadows my present troubles. Calming my fears, they have generated the courage I need to begin planning our escape from the grasp of Matafao.

Sailele beach on Samoa's windward side is
a beautiful place to snorkel and relax.

Which Way Waterfalls 4

"Wow! You can see a long way from up here!" TJ shouts with excitement from atop a thirty foot sheer cliff waterfall.

"Oh my gosh!" I exclaim, jolted from my daydream into the present. "How did you get up there?"

"I just climbed up those tree roots over there. It was easy!" he explains with a serious grin.

"Well, back up from that edge! We don't want to carry you out of here, after you fall," I overreact with caution, trying to regain composure. "What can you see, TJ?" I ask, pointing down the ravine. "Can you see any kind of path, or way out of here from up there?"

"No, there's just a whole lot of trees ... but I can see the ocean," he reports back somberly.

My heart sinks a little. Guess I was hoping for a big exit sign, or at least a visual map of how to get off this volcano.

"Stanley, there's a waterfall down here, too," Joey announces from behind and points down the ravine.

"Really?" I ask with intrigue, "show me!" We wade through a maze of rocks and plants in the stream to reach a fan-shaped waterfall that spills into a blackish pool fifteen feet below. The semicircular rock formation at the top drops straight down, creating a narrow scooping passageway that is slick with moisture. Bridging between the two sides of this steep ravine, it holds us entrapped by its fortification. If we attempt to climb either side, we run the risk of sliding into the funnel and falling on the rocks below.

"Well, that settles that! We aren't going to just walk out of here, like I hoped," I turn to Joey and moan, after looking into the pit. "For all we know, there could be more waterfalls just like this one down there!"

We turn and walk back toward TJ's waterfall, where Sean now stands victoriously at his side. Looking behind them, I can see another smooth-faced cliff. Not as tall as the first, it's probably twenty feet high. But like the first, it spans eighty feet across the gorge where Joey and I stand.

Water shoots out from a single spout at the top of the cliff, as if poured out of a glass pitcher. Then, it spills onto the ledge were TJ and Sean stand, forming the second waterfall beneath them. The cone, we had approached earlier, is visible above the waterfalls to our right. The summit of the volcano can also be seen stretching skyward in the distance. There is flattened area between the two, which wasn't visible from where we approached the cone. Serene in appearance, it has large emergent trees growing across its surface.

From here, Matafao's arch-shaped summit looks like a vertical wall of green, and much less like the end of a sewing needle. It doesn't look climbable. However, the flat area to its right, suggests we could just walk around the massive peak. Some islanders told of another way up Matafao and of a lookout point below the summit, on the backside. *"Perhaps we could walk to the lookout, down to the road, and hail an aiiga bus,"* I envision. *"We'd soon be home, maybe a little later than I thought, but within a reasonable time."*

"Hey guys," I inquire, with a new plan in mind, "are there tree roots we can climb and get to the top of the waterfall behind you?" They immediately investigate and find prop roots, sticking out like spider legs, on a second tree. Asking the boys for directions, Joey and I climb to the top of their waterfall and take our turn viewing the mist-filled valley below. Then, turning back toward the summit, we climb one at a time to the top of the second falls.

Lying on the shelf above, a huge tree trunk extends

itself toward us like a ship's gangplank. We each pull our way through some broken limbs, until we stand triumphantly together, atop the gigantic log. Scoping out the area, we discover this shelf is much larger than the narrow ledge between the two waterfalls. Nearly eighty feet in width, it butts up against the lava-layered base of the summit above. Laterally, it extends across the top of the waterfall for over a hundred feet, before merging with the bottom edge of the vent cone on the other side. At the edge of the shelf, as if cut with a butter-knife, the cone's bare-faced vertical rock metamorphoses into the vine covered features of the waterfall below. From our vantage point, the cone resembles a snug fitting party hat that sits off to one side of Matafao's head.

Near the cone, a water spout shoots out of a volcanic trough and creates the gush of the waterfalls underneath. The dead tree that we stand on is surrounded by a dense thicket of vegetation. Our unobstructed view, from seven feet above the ground, reveals that the thicket covers the shelf from our log all the way to the spout.

"We'll have to go through these bushes," I explain, "and I think we can walk up the bed of the spring when we get over there." At that moment, before I can get out another word, Sean drops to the ground in an attempt to lead the way.

"Ouch!" he shrieks, looking down at his leg, "Oh man, I'm bleeding!"

"How bad?" I ask, without trying to sound alarmed.

"Pretty bad!" he winces from the pain. Grabbing him by the arms, the three of us quickly pull him back upon the log. Though it takes a while to stop the bleeding and several band-aids to cover the wound, we survive our first real injury.

Climbing down carefully, I begin examining the bushes. The lower part of the stem is reed-like with sharp protruding shoots. "That explains Sean's cut— there's no way, we can walk through these!" Disillusioned, my mind begins a desperate search for the answer to our dilemma.

"What'll we do, go back down?" shrugs TJ with some alarm.

In an effort to stall for more time, I mutter, "Just a minute, TJ." And, he seems content with my answer.

Six feet in height and thicker than hair on a dog's back, these plants are a serious barrier. Their thumb-sized stems with sharp blades have grown so close together, it's impossible to separate them and create a path through. Strange as it seems, their tops are fern-like and soft as peach fuzz. Like a magic 8-ball, an idea floats slowly to the top of my head. "It's worth a try," I mutter.

Looking up at the boys with a smile, I lie on my side, and roll up and across the feathery tops of the plants. To our amazement, it is like lying on a featherbed of ferns. The closeness of the stems below, support our weight in the soft tops above. Giggling as boys sometimes do, they roll one after another, until we all stand next to the water spout on the other side of the shelf. This first taste of success causes us to momentarily stare at each other in disbelief. Then with the lingering smiles of circus performers, we begin to examine our new surroundings.

Unlike the rocky stream bed of the ravine, the trough of the spout almost looks man-made. It is nearly two feet wide and eight feet long. Astonishingly, it isn't one single trough; but rather, one trough after another stacked in stair-step fashion up the mountain. About two feet of extremely cold spring water fills each one to overflowing. Encased in solid black volcanic rock, the water has the eerie dark appearance of being bottomless. This illusion makes us question our every step for a while. But as we move up the mountain, cold water rushing past our legs, we eventually relax and begin to investigate once again.

To my surprise, something swims to the surface in front of me. Candy-cane-striped with red and white bands, it looks like a tiny crawfish with long spider-like legs. When it comes up again, I scoop it up with my hands.

"Guys, I just caught a freshwater shrimp!" I exclaim. "How in the world, could it live way up here?" Rushing forward, until we are all standing in a single trough, they curiously examine the catch.

A little further on, something fishlike swims through my legs from behind. Without thinking, I scoop it up as well. Because it is so smooth and slick, I can't hold on to it. But before it slips out of my hands, I get a pretty good look at it. Though barely a foot long, it is a delicacy prized for its taste by nearly all Samoans, a black freshwater eel.

"Wow, Stanley," Sean instructs in a loud voice, "you should have held on to it! You could have sold it for a lot of money!"

"And I suppose you'd carry it back for me, too?" I return in jest, causing the other two boys to giggle. Sean, to our amazement, then turns and starts to walk away in disgust.

"Where are you going?" I demand with some alarm.

"Home!" he replies, as he continues to move down the trough.

In an effort to divert his anger and with all the sincerity I can muster, I ask, "Do you need money for the bus?"

The scowling wrinkles in his face transform into a grin, as he turns, and again joins our troop. Without a word, Joey and TJ smile at each other, as they focus on the watery troughs and wade knee-deep toward the summit above.

In an attempt to soothe the moment and overcome our fatigue, I crank out another story. This time, about seeing an eel prepared for a guest at the Tusi Tala Hotel in Western Samoa. Of course, they know Tusi Tala means "book writer," and is the name the Samoans gave author Robert Louis Stevenson.

"On his island of Savaii," I convey as we walk, "I gave pieces of bread to what I believed to be an unusual fish in a spring-fed pool. When I lured it closer out of the rocks, I could see the fish was several feet long. As you know, eel is a very expensive dish," I tease with a grin. "Maybe I could catch this one?" I add, reaching down and pretending to catch something. "But just about then," I say, looking them directly in the face, "a Samoan sitting near the pool yells, "Don't let it bite you, it is very painful!" And, with eyes bulging, I yank my hand back as if bitten.

Joey immediately leaps out of the water, causing TJ and Sean to burst into laughter. As usual, I can't tell if he is kidding or serious. Regardless, the boys now stare bug-eyed at the spring water, and show no signs of fatigue as they follow close at my heels.

Sooner than I had anticipated, we reach the flat area that we'd seen from below. Under its canopy of a dozen large circumference emergents, and spellbound by a cultivated-looking lawn of ferns, we stand in miniature. As exhaustion begins to take its toll, but before we give way, we stumble toward the towering volcanic plug, reach out in an act of triumph, and touch the myth of Matafao.

While meandering through this forest high above their Island and peering through small openings in the canopy, we view every line of Tutuila's tropical beauty. Pointing at familiar features in the distance, we reach the side of the mountain we had climbed to see. All eyes are suddenly looking in my direction.

"What are we going to do now?" Joey pleads in anguish.

"Well, the bear went over the mountain, to see what he could see," I jest in disappointment. "You know the rest of it!"

The flats, we easily walked, have rolled out into a cockscomb of rock. Like the dorsal fin on a sharks back, the ridge of the cockscomb is so sharp and perilous no trapeze artist could walk it. On its left side, it forms a semicircle drop-off with the vertical face of the summit and plunges a hundred feet into a rocky grave.

Knowing there is no way around the summit, we walk away from the pit and begin to survey the other side of the cockscomb. With some relief, we discover a less intimidating scene. Completely unlike the ravine we came up, at first glance, this valley looks like a gentle scooping slope. Such a change in scenery renews the boy's hopes and initiates a rush to investigate.

Jogging forward with greater enthusiasm, Sean remarks, "It's a slide big enough for King Kong!"

"Yeah, and probably a mile long," I venture a guess. "You see that village down there? It's the one just off the road, about a half mile from where we came up."

"Oh man, Stanley, do you think we can walk down there?" questions Joey, with gung-ho excitement.

"I'm not sure; but I know this, if you fall here, there won't be much left of you by the time you get down there."

"It really does look like you can walk down this slope," I admit, silently in my head. *"However, logic says, it has to be tested ... and not by Joey this time!"* Asking the boys to sit down and stay put, I explain that I'm the only guinea pig in this test.

Nervously looking down the broad slope, I can see that the angle of incline changes. At its start, it is about a 50 degree angle. Though not walkable, it might be climbable. The angle then changes, as it scoops downward, and appears to become walkable. The change in slope doesn't occur for at least a quarter mile down the valley. Unlike the brush-covered ravine Joey slid down, there are many large trees scattered across this surface. The ground vegetation is sparse, almost non-existent. My knowledge as a science teacher is insufficient in understanding this terrain.

"Does the canopy block so much light, that it prevents the production of ground vegetation," I wonder, *"or are the soils too poor?"* The trees suggest a greater depth to the soils, and no spring gouges out a jagged ravine on this side of the mountain. *"Why is this valley so different from the ravine next to it?"*

Looking through the canopy of trees on the downward slope, we can see above the treetops further down the mountain. This allows us to see the village nearly a mile below. Like miniature monopoly houses on a floor, surrounded by tiny tropical fruit trees, the details of the village are easily seen from our vantage point. So much so, I feel embarrassed to be spying on their private lives. It's as if, a walnut grove has been planted between two arms of this volcano, beautiful, but treacherous in terrain!

As I did before, I aim at a large tree below and begin side-stepping down the slope. The ground moves under my feet, but I'm having some success. Reaching the tree some fifty feet below, I look back at the boys. Then, I look down the slope again.

"I can do this, but can they?" I think, as scenarios flash in my mind. *"Like before, one wrong move will mean sliding or tumbling down the incline. How many sharp objects lay at its surface, or just below, ready to rip at*

cloth and flesh?" I agonize. *"Would you gain so much speed, that you couldn't even stop your fall?"*

Slipping with every step, while employing great effort and prayer, I make my way back to the boys. "We're going back down!"

Matafao reveals her volcanic beauty from across Pago Pago Harbor in American Samoa.

A Matai prepares taro for the umu oven, where a pig will be roasted underground.

The view from the flats near the summit of Matafao.

Our open classroom with a view is the
perfect place to tell stories of adventure!

Running the Ravine 5

"Here we go boys, back down to Joey's waterfall," I say looking at my wrist. "My watch has 1:30. We need to move as fast as we can, making sure no one gets hurt."

"Don't worry, Stanley, our parents know we're with you," Sean declares with a thoughtful expression.

Already climbing ahead, Joey tries to encourage with, "Yeah, we're still having fun too!"

Wading, rolling, and climbing, while concentrating only on the terrain, we make our way to the lower waterfall. We stand and stare at the gut of the open-sided funnel; its upper torso has a much rougher texture than we remember. The irregular surface creates footholds and handholds that would allow us to climb at least halfway into its watery chest.

As spring water falls down over its face, it becomes a fountain of silver tears that spray out of the blackish pool below. The intimidating dark water at its bottom suggests a pool of some depth; but I'm reminded, how the watery troughs above had deceived me. Base tones bellowing from the fountain below also indicate this is no shallow pool.

"What I wouldn't give for some rope," I blurt out with some despair. My machete seems to only add weight to my arms. This backpack, like a trash can of empty containers, produces hot humid sweat that continually rolls down my spine. Squatting low, I splash some cool water on my face in an attempt to clear my head. "There just isn't an easy way down."

Handing my backpack and machete to the boys, I begin scaling down the one flat side of the funnel. When I reach the half-way point, possibly nine feet from the pool, I run out of handholds. Staring at the pool below, I convince myself of the obvious, "I'll have to jump." Picking a deep looking spot, close to the center of the pool, I leap from the ledge. My feet meet the water with a splash and instantly ski out from under me. With a sharp pain, my tailbone skips off a hard surface; and with a thud, my head slips under the water. Fearing the worst, I remain submerged and motionless hoping the cold water will cause the pain to subside. Soon, due to a need for oxygen and a resurrection for the boys' sake, I surface without revealing my situation.

"Are you alright, Stanley?" I hear the boys say with some laughter, when I finally rise for air.

Unsure of the answer, I stand upright in only four feet of water. Other than a throbbing in my head, ankles, and backside, I seem to have weathered the fall unscathed! "Give me a minute," I plead, as the boys turn and try to hide their giggles.

Stumbling, while trying to compose myself, I search for my next step. Wading toward the waterfall, I discover a giant rock just beneath the splash of the falls. Luckily, I had hit the mammoth sized marble on a downward sloping edge. Like a park slide, it had thrust me forward into deeper water. Had I aimed at the waterfall's splash, where the water above the rock was no more than six inches deep, I could have easily broken a bone or two. Peering toward heaven, I thank my maker. Then, looking into the boys eyes, I confidently ask, "Who's next?"

Evidently, I made a bigger splash than I thought; because the boys, quickly turn and try to become invisible in the jungle. Ignoring their camouflage, I search for deeper water. Between the funnel wall and the enormous submerged rock the water is about five feet deep. Again, I ask for a volunteer.

"Climb down to where I jumped using the hand holds. From that point, you'll need to turn and jump to a spot in front of me," I explain. "As you land, catch my arms with yours. That way, I can help cushion your fall into the water. The bottom under my feet has a lot of loose gravel, and with this much water, you'll land soft," I assure them.

TJ, with the proof of his bravery, walks gallantly around the top of the waterfall. With a determined look, but without saying a word, he begins descending the ledge. Running out of footholds, he turns into a launch position. Jumping for the target, he makes his splashdown to safety. With that and a little more coaxing, Sean and Joey eventually follow his example. The excitement of the jump and the relief of our success produce more laughter … some at my expense. Nevertheless, we have beaten the obstacles. We are again wading down the ravine, a determined troop.

Now more relaxed, I begin to daydream as we walk. My thoughts drift into the classroom, where I'm reminded of my good fortune. These island kids love investigating new things, studying the thoughts of people in ancient cultures, and learning what life is like in the rest of the world. Every morning as my students enter the classroom, one or more will ask, "What are you going to teach us today, Stanley?"

What more could a teacher ask for? And yet, as a biologist, it becomes my responsibility to teach them about the living organisms on their island and especially about their preservation. Discovering the similarities, between human anatomy and that of other living forms, almost always creates compassion for life.

For that reason, though it might sound strange, my students perform many classroom dissections.

Here on the island, I don't have access to dissection specimens. But with my students, that isn't a problem. "If we were back in the States, we would be dissecting frogs as we cover this chapter," I said one day in class.

"Oh, Stanley, we have no frogs on island, but we have big toads," a student responded immediately.

"They have poison glands on their backs. Could we still dissect them?" another added, causing us all to wonder.

"Well, what if we just turn them over on their back," I asked. "That's how we need to dissect them anyway?" They nodded in agreement; and the next day, there were five large toads on my desk. We spent the morning sitting in a fale', shaded by a roof of coconut fronds, looking at body organs, and sharing ideas.

"I'm living in paradise!" I sigh from my daydream, as we wind our way down the ravine.

Before now, like most people, I had viewed paradise as sitting on a tropical beach, drink in hand, and listening to ocean waves without a care. But what about these kids, they live on a tropical island every day? Out of curiosity, I had asked my students to write a paragraph entitled, *"What Paradise Means to Me."* Though sitting in a classroom with a tropical view, every student, without exception, wrote about the same desire: *"If I could find a way to attend college in the states, I could find a job that would allow me to buy my own car, and have my own home."* Not one of them wrote about living on this beautiful tropical island of Tutuila. To my shame, I realized for the first time, I had been living in paradise all my life!

The slippery rocks underfoot again focus my attention on the task at hand. My spirits renewed, it feels good to be here, walking with my boys down this ravine. *"We're not lost— this is their home! What stories they'll tell,"* I think, trying to envision our return to the classroom. *"With all its difficulties, this day will certainly stand out as one of my best."*

Even though we can only see the plants and spring bed just ahead, we're making progress back to civilization, and the ravine keeps getting wider. Picking up the pace, we begin to talk about places each of us has explored on the island. It seems like a good time to lighten the moment with another story.

"Let me tell you about the pearl shell, large enough to cover my whole belly, I had to throw away," I begin. "On the back side of the island, I swam a quarter mile across a bay, just to explore a cave that was visible on the other side. On the way back, I found a huge scalloped shell. You know, like mermaids are supposed to live in," I say with a smile and a wink. "Even without a mermaid, it was so bulky, I had to use one whole arm to hold it across my belly. Swimming with my other arm, while staring at the bottom, the ocean waves began to feel like a carnival ride of regurgitation! And along with my lunch, I finally tossed it," I groan, sticking out my tongue. "Never thought crawling onto a beach could feel so much like success!"

"Oh no! Not another one!" Sean yells from ahead, terminating my moment of humor.

With disbelief, another twenty foot waterfall drains our energy and the ledge we stand on. No footholds, no pool, just a smooth, half-cylinder tube plummeting straight down to a rocky floor. My brain, as if filled with all the bubble gum I ever swallowed, grinds to a halt. "Now what?" I sputter in disgust.

"Hey, there's a cave over here!" TJ calls out from the left, as he waves his arms to get our attention. "I can see some light down at the bottom! Maybe we can go through here?"

Unknowingly, while my big mouth had been running, the terrain had been changing. Large black boulders are scattered along the stream bed. And for the first time, a black barricade of rock, the size of a house, blocks most of the ravine. Sitting on the ledge where we stand, it has an odd cyclopean hole in its face. With its sinister attachment to the waterfall at our side, like an obstructing dam, it blocks the whole valley. *"But, what if this really is the daylight we've been looking for? Surely, we deserve a break!"*

"You can really see light," I ask in disbelief, "it goes all the way through?"

"I don't know? Come and see!" TJ invites, pointing at the entrance.

Making my way to the entrance, I manuever into position and take a look. *There's light down there alright,* I agree, *with a long tapering tunnel and a low ceiling. It doesn't reveal its' opening at the other end. But, as far as I can see, it is passable.* Could this discovery actually be the doorway to our road home?

When surrounded by humid jungle in the lower
ravine, take time to cool-off in the spring!

Anchored strong by its' prop roots, I stand in
miniature, under a giant emergent tree!

Caving In and Antics Out 6

Dark and damp with mosses and ferns growing near the putrid stench of its mouth, this black hole is offering us a ticket out. Whether an igneous rock-pile left here from an ancient landslide or an opening from which Matafao exhaled her volcanic gases, this cave is millennia old. With its dull, rough finish, flattened ceilings, and weathered walkway, this opening has all the enticing entrapments of a limestone cave back home. Though lacking stalactite and stalagmite formations, this black igneous rock, fire-made from magma, still has a familiar friendly feel.

From stooped positions, we move wide-eyed and alert into the abyss. Our eyes struggling to focus, we examine every shadow in detail. A distant dim light draws us ever deeper into the muddy throat, until we are crouched, as if ducks walking a faint moonlit path.

After some 25 feet of duck walking, my legs turn to stumps, and my ears begin to ring. The race isn't over, but my body is locking up. In desperation, I reach down and grab my ankles, hoping my arms still have some reserve. To my surprise, the problem isn't just my legs. It appears, there's at least six inches of mud beneath me.

"No wonder my feet won't move!" I think. *"And that ringing sound appears to be coming from over my head?"* Looking up, I see a ceiling completely covered by a hundred bats! Each one communicating with a squeak of echo location, while wearing their best vampire smile! *"That can't be good!"* Bat isn't a language I speak, but I have no trouble interpreting their meaning.

Motioning for silence, I point up at the ceiling, and the boys quickly interpret my meaning. Wasting no time, they make a determined exit. With renewed vigor, followed by grotesque sucking sounds, I free my feet from the six inches of bat guano that holds me motionless. Racing into daylight, a much faster duck, I gulp a breath of fresh air.

Though another chilling experience, a spring water bath never felt so good! Cleaning off the face of my waterproof watch, I discover it's already 4:30. Nevertheless, the adrenaline rush from the cave blew the cobwebs out of my head and makes this ravine a welcomed sight.

Observation may be what I teach, but with my dogs barking and my aching tailbone tucked between my legs, I missed a huge detail. Next to the downspout, opposite the cave, stands a dead "Samoan Christmas Tree." Neither a pine tree, nor used for the same purpose, it still has the very festive shape of short limbs spiraling upward around a single trunk. Striking it with my machete, it vibrates with a seasoned hard pitch.

Towering some 25 feet in the air, and obviously dead, it's perfect for our purposes. Asking the boys to stand back, I begin hacking at its trunk.

"What are you doing now, Stanley?" Sean impatiently questions with a raised eyebrow.

"This is our way down Sean," I respond and continue notching out the cut; even though I know, they probably think I've gone "Batty".

Either the wood is really hard or I am really tired, because twice I stop to catch my breath. But after a time, it topples upside down over the edge. Falling like a hinged door, it becomes a perfect ladder, leading to the rocky floor below.

"Oh, I get it!" says Sean, as he grabs the tree and prepares to climb down.

"Wait a minute Sean," I caution while gasping for air.

"You can go first, but let the three of us get hold of it, so it can't roll over." As he climbs into the branches, I add, "Test each dead limb with a foot before you put your weight on it. Let's make sure, we get out of this ravine in one piece."

In no time, all four of us are down on the lower shelf with a new bounce in our step. Like conquerors, we follow the mountain stream as it journeys toward our exit. Soon, however, ripples in the pool at our feet indicate a tropical shower is on the way. Darkened by clouds overhead, the cooling jungle begins to fill with fog. The eerie backdrop generates an uncomfortable feeling in my gut. With it comes the frightening realization, that in less than two hours, we will be struggling by starlight. In the tropics, like clockwork, daylight is always twelve hours long. No daylight savings time here, if we haven't made our escape by 6pm, we will be groping in darkness.

"Hey, Stanley!" TJ smiles, as he catches a few raindrops in his mouth.

Turning toward the other two, I notice Joey cupping his hands in a small waterfall to catch a drink.

"I wouldn't do that, Joey," I warn with a stern jaw.

"Why not? We drink rainwater off our roof at home!" he counters.

It's true, many island homes have guttering systems

that pour rainwater into large concrete cisterns, which serve as family water towers.

"Yeah, but this water probably has bat poop in it!" exclaims Sean, scrunching up his face, as if he just came out of the cave. Joey quickly slings the water out of his hands and shakes his head, causing us to snicker at his animation.

"Remember the day we looked at water from that old bucket close to the school?" I ask. "It looked like it was clean, until we put it under the microscope."

"Yeah, it had all those little bugs swimming in it," Joey acknowledges with a shrug.

"That's why we can't drink this water," I add. "We'll be out of here soon, and you can drink all you want." Then the jailer rattles my chain, *"They haven't had a drink since the coconuts, over six hours ago."* Cringing, I try to reassure myself, *"We can't have that far to go …"*

"What about those bats?" I ask, trying to counter both the rain and our thirst.

"They weren't really very big, like flying foxes," replies Sean with a smirk.

"Yeah, I see big ones all the time, just at dark," Joey adds swinging his arms as he walks.

"Have to admit, that was a little scary back there,"

TJ confesses, as he lunges forward to get in the conversation.

"Did you guys see the fruit bats at the Farm and Food Fair?" Sean inquires with big eyes.

"That reminds me, fruit bats are eating the papaya off my trees, before I can," I interrupt with a frown.

"One evening last week, I was walking down the road to the bus stop and heard this loud, "SWOOSH! SWOOSH!" coming from behind me. When I turned around, right over my head, there was five foot of bat wing on what appeared to be a mad Chihuahua. Didn't know my head looked so much like a papaya?" I grin.

"I could have told you that Stanley." Sean retaliates with a serious face, causing all three them to burst into laughter.

Biting my tongue, I conclude, *"It must be my turn to eat crow, which is better than bat, any day?*

As the clouds overhead thin and allow more light to filter through, we can see the valley opening wider. With very few plants growing along its surface, the streambed is almost a solid sheet of rock under our feet. Slick and wet, it becomes a comical dance floor, both entertaining and inhibiting to our forward progress. Spattering water in every direction, the boys run and slide, as if on ice.

Extending from one side of the ravine to the other,

this smooth rock forms tier after tier of three-foot waterfalls. Dropping off in uniform steps, they appear to lead into some giant's secret garden. Spellbound, we stop to peer from one of the shelves. And for the first time, since the upper falls, we have a panoramic view of what lies ahead.

Like gigantic prehistoric "pickup sticks," massive black tree trunks are strewn across the valley in our pathway. Beyond them, in the distance, the ocean waves and gains our full attention. Jumping from the steps, we approach the challenge of this colossal log-jam. Nearly as thick in diameter, as we are tall, their dark, damp trunks become petrified roadblocks. Seeing them as another slippery obstacle we must defeat, we crawl under some, and boost ourselves over others. Our progress is slow, but our determination never higher!

With evening's looming darkness, less than an hour away, the valley finally opens wide and gently rolls off into the foreground. The boys begin to run downhill toward the roadway, leaving me far behind.

"Slow down, we've made it!" I admonish, though inwardly sharing their excitement. "Don't fall and get hurt now!" Then in the distance, and just as sudden as they had begun, they come to a complete stop.

"Holy mackerel, what'll we do now!" Sean wails, as if in pain.

Like an uncontrollable nightmare, the welcomed view

from the giant steps above, has changed itself into a monstrous terminal waterfall. A waterfall, though small in flow, drops a hundred feet straight down. Forming a tangled, vine-covered cliff, it extends itself from one side of the ravine to the other.

Standing at its edge, we look hopelessly at houses along the roadway below. In shame, I turn to the boys and confess, "I know where we are. I should have known this is where the ravine would lead. See the store right down there?" I ask, pointing at its location. "That's the store across the road from Coconut Point."

"Look, Stanley," Joey interrupts, "there's a guy coming out of the store! Hey! Hey!" he yells with all his might.

"Joey, don't yell!" I insist. "What's he going to do, go get a hundred foot ladder? We still have over half an hour before it gets dark. We can find another way out by ourselves."

Though said with force, hearing those words come out of my mouth sends shockwaves through my resolve. In an attempt to bring all our attention back to the problem at hand, I walk away from the waterfall. The path, we came up this morning, is somewhere on top of the left side of this valley. Walking in that direction, we are forced to confront the volcanic arm that led us up Matafao, held us captive in the ravine, formed the deadly drop-off at our right, and now stretches its face into the valley, where it has us completely bewildered.

Upon investigation we notice, its features are nothing like the steep jungle-covered slope Joey rode to the bottom. This slope is covered by giant emergent trees. Trees with prop roots, like those we had climbed back at the upper falls. With renewed enthusiasm, Sean and TJ run ahead to the tree nearest the valley floor. Using the prop roots like a jungle gym, they climb to its uphill side. In awe, Joey and I watch as they try to make it to the next tree by climbing on all fours. But to our frustration, like the slip-n-slide we've been on all day, they slide back to the lower tree with a groan. The disappointment that pours from their eyes extinguishes our all our hopes.

"Wait a minute, Stanley!" Joey exclaims. "Remember that picture in our book with the army ants crossing a stream? What if we did that?" Like light-bulbs in our head, the idea conceived illuminates our faces like glowing jack-o-lanterns. *"It could work!"*

With darkness coming on, Joey and I quickly climb around the tree toward the other two boys. By the time we get there, Sean has deciphered the plan, and has instructed TJ to lay face-down toward the tree above them. In turn, he climbs further up the hill, using TJ as a human ladder. Putting his feet on TJ's shoulders, he lays face-down above him, and waits for Joey's move up the ladder.

Once in place, the three boys stretch out like a rope, nearly fifteen feet up the slope. Last to scale, using the boys' clothes for handholds, I make my way to Joey's shoulders. The next tree is still a little beyond my reach. With a belly-buster lunge, I grab one of its prop-roots, and the boys ecstatically cheer. Then, forgetting they still hug a slippery slope, each attempts to stand. In what looks like a three-man mud-wrestling match, they fall into a dog pile on the slope.

"Hold up!" I giggle from my position in the section ladder. "Get back into position, start with TJ at the bottom, and climb up the ladder one person at a time." Finally, as the last link, I pull myself into the inverted basket of prop roots of the second tree. Before I can even circumnavigate the tree, the boys are again laid out in antlike fashion toward the next tree.

After five ant bridges and a change in terrain, the boys walk in gorilla fashion, on all fours, to the top of the ridge. Searching for the pathway we came up, they quickly find such a trail. Though not positive it's the one, believing all paths lead to the road, they ask for permission to run ahead.

With darkness close at hand and time running out, getting home anytime soon means catching that last Aiga bus leaving Pago Pago harbor. When the fisheries close at 5pm, family buses take all the workers home. That last bus, the six o'clock ride out of Pago going west, will most likely be loading out this very minute. *We must catch that bus!*

Trying to keep up with the boys is impossible. My legs really have become stump-like this time. Every tree root on the path becomes a hurdle to cross. Stubbing my toe on one after another, I'm hurled to the ground time and time again. Sean returns to check on the slower stiff-legged progress of his teacher and offers help.

"I'm ok," I insist, though wishing he could help. "You need to get down there and help Joey stop that bus." He bolts down the trail and is soon out of sight; and I follow, in my drop and roll fashion.

As the trails ends, one last obstacle raises its head. A scooping cut-out of the hillside offers a short mudslide of about twenty feet onto the shoulder of the road. At this point, it looks like a kiddy ride, to accomplished mud wrestlers like these boys. When at last I arrive, they watch me tumble safely down; then they lift me out of the ditch, until the four of us stand in the middle of the road.

"Here it comes!" Joey shouts like a foghorn from the middle of the road.

The bus headlights meander snakelike, appearing and disappearing, in and out of ocean inlets, as we watch with anticipation. Though disconcerting, by necessity, a road around volcanic mountains must follow the curvature of the flat shoreline.

Eventually, it makes the last turn and onto our stretch of road. Waving our arms frantically in the headlights, we can see the illuminated passengers staring back at us, from inside. The bus stops, the door swings open, and we enthusiastically hand the driver our twenty-five cent fares.

To our surprise, the Samoans on one side of the bus, after having worked all day at the fisheries, stand up and move to the other side. *"How nice is that,"* I think, always impressed by their kindness.

We each sit down, with a sigh of relief, in our own seat. With every eye looking at us from across the bus, a Samoan elder partially stands, and with a look of compassion leans toward the boys.

"Where have you been?" he asks in a low inquisitive voice.

Without hesitation, Sean responds with a voice of conquest, "We've been on Matafao!"

Then, with a low, nearly subsonic whisper, somewhere between horror and awe, the elder echoes, "Oh-h-h! Matafao!"

Each worker's face transforms in amazement, as with great pride, I turn and look at the boys.

"They did it. They stuck together and got off that mountain," I reflect.

It's like I'm looking at them for the first time. Well, at least for the first time since we started down that ravine. With a reawakened consciousness, I see them more clearly. They are nearly covered with mud, probably mixed with a little bat guano, as the air in the bus would suggest. Their faces are smudged like Rambo, and a collection of debris garnishes their hair, collars, and pockets.

Turning with apprehension, a face appears in the window! I barely recognize my own reflection. It isn't just the mud on my face. It's an expression, one I've never seen, "somewhere between horror and awe."

"See, Stanley," Joey slices the silence, "I told you—no one ever goes up there!"

Turning toward the window to hide a smile, my reflection reappears. But this time, I see the reassurance of a calming twinkle in my eye.

Each year on Flag Day, the Samoan people sing and dance as they celebrate their American heritage.

Further Readings

A teacher's mantra by Robert Louis Stevenson might read: "Don't judge each day by the harvest you reap, but by the seeds you plant." This book follows his advice and contains a multitude of scientific terms and information, which I hope serve as being both entertaining and educational. Stevenson wrote books about his *Treasure Island*, being *Kidnapped* at sea, and even about the dueling personalities of *Jekyll and Hyde*. He not only wrote about such adventures, but was able to live out his own adventure from his island home in Western Samoan.

Jules Verne, on the other hand, masterfully wrote about mystical adventures such as submarines that dive *Twenty Thousand Leagues Under the Sea*, going *Around the World in Eighty Days*, or going *In Search of the Castaways* on the other side of the world. Writing from his imagination, he created such adventures, before ever leaving the comforts of France and Europe. Later, however, he was able to sail around Europe in his own ship and write further of a *Mysterious Island*, with incredible creatures created by a crazed captain.

Taking us a step further, H.G. Wells allows us to travel with him in his *Time Machine*, or to fight off alien invaders in his *War of the Worlds*. Just like Leonardo de Vinci's drawings three hundred years earlier, stories such as these have inspired readers to explore life's possibilities, reach into their imaginations, and pull forth the inventions of a better future.

Postscript

"**A** *man should stop his ears against the paralyzing terror, and run the race that is set before him with a single mind,*" said Robert Louis Stevenson. Good advice for getting off volcanic mountains. Yet, it would be many years after Matafao, before I would discover these words. On the other hand, discoveries in technology during that time have made it possible to reconnect with Joey and Sean (via Facebook) and laugh about our adventure. This book might even make a reunion with classmates and their families a reality ... on flatter ground, of course!

Sadly, my tenure as a volunteer teacher in American Samoa only lasted one year. Although my wife and I were down to our last $20 on the flight home, we were wearing million-dollar smiles. When we arrived back in Texas, a summer school position provided an audience for the first telling of this story. The students loved it so, that some begged to accompany me, if ever I returned to Tutuila. Since then, the telling and retelling of the story has kept it fresh in my mind.

I'm sure Joey, Sean, and TJ will have additions that only they could have seen from their vantage points. With great anticipation, I look forward to hearing their remembrances after they have read my own.

The people of Samoa love to be called Americans. Their generosity and affection for missionaries, who come to share life with them on their island, is immeasurable. When leaving the island, those who have touched their hearts are given gifts of handmade treasures, as they have been for hundreds of years. It is my wish, that this book will somehow be a benefit to their island home and their way of life. Perhaps, it will encourage readers to visit the beautiful Samoan Islands. And by stepping out of their comfort zone and stretching forth a generous hand, they too might comprehend the good fortune that Robert Louis Stevenson must have found on his *Treasure Island*.

Surviving Rip Tides

What I learned about rip tides, by accident, can save many lives. Many people caught in near shore currents will drown while trying to swim out of the current. The method commonly given for survival involves swimming vigorously parallel to the shore until out of the rip current. This method makes two assumptions that could easily cause fatality.

The first assumption is that the person in trouble can actually swim some distance to safety, while being swept into deeper water by the currents. Yet, many beach goers who get caught in currents are not good swimmers. Many, think the bottom will always be just below them and believe they can easily wade back to shore. When caught in rip currents, poor swimmers most often panic for lack of a plan. Believing their only way out is to vigorously swim, they quickly fatigue and drown. But, what if all it took to survive was the ability to float?

Another false assumption occurs when a wall of churning water is formed by an outgoing tide meeting incoming waves. The outgoing tide creates both an undertow that pulls you out to sea and a churning wall where the shelf drops off into deeper ocean. Churning water can push a swimmer under, even as they try to fight their way to the surface. Without a plan, poor swimmers are again doomed. But, this wall of water can be avoided by those who learn to float in the uppermost strata of water. When pushed toward the shore by the sea breeze that is always present during daylight hours, they can easily overcome the danger with a simple backstroke.

One exception should be noted. If storm winds are blowing seaward, no swimmer should be in the water! Under such conditions, if caught in an outgoing current, another strategy must be attempted. Under such conditions, swimmers must face even greater fears. But, there is time to prepare for what must be done. While restfully floating toward the churning wall of water, the swimmer should exhale many times in an attempt to exchange the carbon dioxide in their lungs for all the oxygen they can hold. Near the ocean floor, the rip current moves seaward with great force, and flows underneath the churning wall. By taking a deep breath and swimming or at least sinking to the bottom, the swimmer allows the rip current to take them under the churning wall. Returning to a floating position, they can then begin to yell for help, while waiting for rescuers. Their greatest obstacle may be overcoming the fear of floating in deep water! You can do this; your life is on the line!

Note: I've been telling this story to classes for years, even when the students didn't live anywhere near the ocean. Now, floating is slowly becoming part of the published survival strategies. NOAA has included floating as another possible option for those that are not good swimmers. Even as I'm writing these strategies in the summer of 2012, two young girls have indeed survived deadly currents by floating until rescuers could reach them. Please help get the word out!

Glossary of Terms

Website: National Park of American Samoan ww.nps.
gov/npsa/index.htn

Admonish: to instruct someone what is important to
know

Aiga: (ah-ing-ah) is the word for family, such as family
bus

American Samoa: an island group in the Pacific Ocean
that the USA has protected since 1899.

Bolster: build up, make stronger

Buttress: prop or support by using long horizontal
braces

Canopy: an umbrella shape formed overhead by the
leaves and branches of the treetops

Captivating: attention getting or charming

Catastrophe: utter failure or a bad ending

Chat piles: the gravel left over from crushing rock that is piled near the crusher

Circumnavigate: go completely around

Coaxing: to ask someone with kind words to do it your way

Cockscomb: a volcanic formation that resembles the comb on a rooster head

Dissection: to cut something down the middle so the internal structure can be seen

Emergents: trees in the rain forest which grow tall enough to extend above the canopy

Encompassing: surrounding or completely covering

Fale: (fall-lay) the Samoan word for an open-air house, usually made of poles which hold up a roof of leaves.

Flying foxes: the largest bats in the world, known as fruit bats because of their diet

Foliage: the leaves and flowers of plants that makes them colorful

Gig: a sharp fork-shaped spear used to catch fish or frogs in the water

Gouges: indented, irregular shapes in a surface that look as if dug out by hand

Guano: poop

Herbaceous: normally small plants without roots or stems that have vessels to carry water up the plant

Igneous rock: rocks from molten materials in the Earth's surface, like lava and magma.

Intrigue: to stir the imagination and cause interest or curiosity

Inverted: turned upside down

Machete': a cutting tool with one large knifelike blade used to cut sugar cane or brush

Magma: molten material in the earth which when cooled forms volcanic rock

Matafao: (Mata-fa-ow) *as in the word now;* is the highest peak on the island of Tutuila, American Samoa

Matai: (mah-tie) the Samoan word for chief, a place of honor in the family or tribe.

Meander: to wind around in a snakelike pattern

Mesmerized: to stare, as if hypnotized

Millennia: a thousand years

Monopoly Game: a game played by rolling dice to determine moves around the board

Ominous: breath-taking or fateful moment

Ozarks: mountains in the central states of Missouri and Arkansas

Pago Pago: (pong-oh pong-oh) the capital of American Samoan located in the world's largest natural harbor

Palagi: (pah-long-ee) means from gates of Heaven and is used by the Samoan's for white people

Petrified: hardened into rock by absorbing mineral water

Plinko game: discs dropped in the top, hit pins on the way down, changing the bin they can land in at the bottom

Putrid: having the smell of decayed material

Regurgitation: to throw swallowed material back up into the throat

Sailele: (sigh-lay-lay) perhaps the most beautiful sandy beach on the isle of Tutuila

Samoan Alphabet: having only 14 letters, it has all 5 vowels, but only 9 consonants.

Spelunker: one who explores caves

Stalactites: inverted cone- shaped formations on the ceilings of damp caves produced from minerals in the water

Stalagmites: cone-shaped formations on cave floors produced by mineral water dripping from the ceiling

Subsonic: sounds lower in pitch than the human ear can hear

Tailings: the gravel left behind after desired minerals have be extracted from rock

Terrestrial: on land or living on land

Treacherous: dangerous or difficult to attempt on foot

Trough: a U-shaped formation or channel

Tutuila: the principle and largest island of the American Samoan Islands; 17 miles long, and approx. 5 miles wide

Vegetation: the plant material in a given area, such as grass, trees, etc

Volcanic plug: magma cooled into rock that plugs a volcanic vent when the eruption subsides

Weathered: eroded or worn away by wind, water, and changing temperature.